SIGN: JYAGA MARU KUN

PUTTING THAT ASIDE...

...BUSINESS IS BOOMING.

STEP 58 ▸▸ FOREBODING ENTANGLEMENTS

HE SEEMED INTERESTED IN THAT CHILD OF YOURS, BELL CRANELL...
I CAN'T HELP BUT FEEL HE'S PLANNING SOMETHING.
CURSES! I HAD NO IDEA MASCOTS MAKE SUCH A DIFFERENCE...
HMM... AREN'T YOU GOING TOO FAR?
HERMES DOESN'T SEEM LIKE THE TYPE TO STIR UP TROUBLE.
WELL, THAT MAY BE.
...BUT SOMETHING FEELS DIFFERENT THIS TIME.
...ANY REASON WHY?
DIVINE INTUITION.
KA (FLASH)
...I SEE...
THOUGH NOTHING'S AS UNCONVINCING AS DIVINE INTUITION...
IN ANY CASE, YOUR CHILD JUST ENTERED THE MIDDLE LEVELS.
WATCH OVER HIM WELL DURING THIS PERILOUS TIME, HESTIA.
I WILL. THANKS, TAKÉ.
AREN'T YOUR CHILDREN IN THE MIDDLE LEVELS TOO?
INDEED. WE BOTH NEED TO STAY ALERT.

SO, ASFI...
...WHAT CAN YOU TELL ME ABOUT *HIM*?
ACCORDING TO THE PUBLIC INFORMATION AT THE GUILD, HE HAS REACHED FLOOR TWELVE, HERMES-SAMA.
DID HE NOW? MAYBE HE'S GONE OFF TO THE MIDDLE LEVELS?
I'D EXPECT NOTHING LESS FROM THE RECORD HOLDER. VERY FAST.
I HAVE ALSO CONFIRMED HE POSSESSES POWERFUL MAGIC.
STRONG ENOUGH TO BEAT AN INFANT DRAGON IN ONE SHOT.
...BUT THAT'S NOT THE ONLY THING.
HMM?
THERE ARE ALSO REPORTS HE BOUGHT ENOUGH SALAMANDER WOOL TO EQUIP A PARTY.

WORD IS HE MANAGED TO SLAY A MINOTAUR...
...BECAUSE HE WAS LUCKY ENOUGH TO HIT AN INJURED ONE WITH SAID MAGIC BEFORE LOKI FAMILIA COULD FINISH THE JOB...
SOME ADVENTURERS GO SO FAR AS TO CALL HIM THE "PHONY ROOKIE."
HA-HA-HA-HA! "PHONY ROOKIE"! THAT'S GOT A NICE RING TO IT!
BUT...
HE *ONLY* MANAGED TO BEAT IT WITH HIS MAGIC, HE *ONLY* DELIVERED THE FINAL BLOW...
A GOD'S BLESSING ISN'T SO EASILY FOOLED...
...BY SUCH CHEAP JUDGMENTS...
I BELIEVE THESE RUMORS REFLECT DISBELIEF PERTAINING TO HIS INCREDIBLY FAST LEVEL UP...
AHH, THAT MAKES SENSE.
ADVENTURERS ARE ALWAYS SO HARD ON EACH OTHER.
...ARE YOU PLANNING SOMETHING FOR THE LITTLE ROOKIE?

WHAT'S THIS, ASFI? FEELING JEALOUS BECAUSE I HAVEN'T BEEN AROUND?
ZUI (GLARE)
HARDLY!

BA (FWIP)
I'M SAYING I'VE HAD ENOUGH OF DEALING WITH YOUR MESSES!
THE WHOLE FAMILIA IS GRATEFUL TO YOU. AS THEIR LEADER, IT'S THANKS TO YOU THEY HAVE IT SO EASY.
SU (SHF)
EVEN I COUNT ON YOU A LOT.
TRUSTED BY YOUR FRIENDS AND YOUR GOD—

PON
PON (PAT)
HA-HA! THIS MUST BE WHAT THEY CALL "THE PERKS OF THE JOB"!
ZURI (TREMBLE)
...I HATE THIS.

KUI (PUSH)
...HAVE YOU MADE CONTACT WITH HESTIA FAMILIA?
NO, NOT YET.
KOHON (COUGH)
ZAA (SCUFF)
BE-FORE THAT...
...I NEED TO HAVE A TALK WITH A CERTAIN **SOMEONE**.
豊穣の女主人
SIGN: THE BENEVOLENT MISTRESS
...

GIII (CREAK)
MEWLCOME!

...MEOW? HERMES-SAMA?
OH! IT'S BEEN TOO LONG, CHLOE-CHAN!

SORRY, BUT WOULD YOU GET MIA FOR ME?
BISHI (SNAP)
YES, SIR, MEOW! JUST A MEOW-MENT!
—HOLD IT!
DAN (STOMP)

WHAT'S A GOD DOIN' BARGIN' IN HERE IN THE MIDDLE OF THE DAY?
NO NEED TO GET ANGRY, MIA.
IT'S RUINING YOUR PRETTY FACE.
BACHIN (BING)
ANY
MORE
JOKIN'
N' I'LL
IP OFF
YER
EAD!!
IF YA GOT BUSINESS, THEN OUT WITH IT!
I'M BUSY.
KA
KA (STEP)
OKAY, GETTING TO THE POINT—
I'D LIKE TO MAKE AN APPOINTMENT WITH FREYA-SAMA.

... HMPH!
FUI (TURN)
I'M NO MESSENGER FOR FOOLISH GODS.
YA GOT FEET. USE 'EM IF YA WANNA SPEAK TO HER THAT BAD.
WELL, THAT DIDN'T WORK.
DON'T LOOK AT ME.
...HERMES-SAMA?
GIII (CREAK)
OH! IF IT ISN'T SYR-CHAN!

IT'S BEEN SO LONG! HOW YA BEEN?
PAAA (BEAM)
IT HAS BEEN A WHILE.
I'M GLAD TO SEE YOU ARE WELL.
AHH, WELL-MANNERED CITY GIRLS REALLY ARE THE BEST!
HOW ABOUT IT, SYR-CHAN? CARE FOR A DATE WITH YOURS TRULY!?
HEE HEE. I MUST RESPECTFULLY DECLINE THE INVITATION.
MY HEART IS IN NEED OF CONSOLING...
OUCH! OW, OW, OW!?
STOP THAT, ASFI! MY EAR CAN'T TAKE IT!!
GYUUU (PULL)
NOW, WOULD YOU CARE TO HAVE A SEAT...?
UM, HERMES-SAMA?
SUTA
SUTA
SUTA (STEP)
SUTA

DOSU (PLOP)
SYR-CHAN. MIND IF I ASK YOU SOMETHING?
SURE... WHAT IS IT?
THAT'S BELL-SAN'S USUAL SEAT...
KNOW ANYTHING ABOUT BELL CRANELL?
I'D LIKE TO HEAR ANYTHING AND EVERYTHING YOU'VE GOT.
PIKUN (TWITCH)

......
WHY WOULD YOU ASK ME A QUESTION LIKE THAT?
WELL, I HEARD HE'S A REGULAR HERE.
CHIRARI (GLANCE)
AND I'M RATHER INTERESTED IN THE LITTLE ROOKIE.
WHAT? I'M NOT GONNA DO ANYTHING STRANGE.
NI (GRIN)
SO, HOW 'BOUT IT?

THERE'S NOTHING I WANT TO TELL YOU AT THIS TIME, HERMES-SAMA.
YOU DON'T TRUST ME?
NOPE.
NOT EVEN A LITTLE BIT.
NIKKOU (SMILE)
にこぉ
VERY WISE.

MEAN-
WHILE—
DUNGEON
"MIDDLE
LEVELS"
FLOOR
THIRTEEN

KYUI!!
!
AL-
MIRAJ
...!!
OOO
(WHOOSH)
EVERY-
ONE,
STAY
ALERT...
...
KYUI!!
KII!!

GI
(GRIP)

BA (RUSH)
BUON (THROW)
GYARURU (SPIN)
DOFUU (THUD)

BUBAA
(SPLAT)
CHI...
CHIGUSA-DONO!

REMAIN CALM, MIKOTO!
SEE TO HER WOUND!
DO (THUMP)
SOMEONE FROM THE CENTER, FORWARD! COVER CHIGUSA'S SPOT!
DADA (DASH)
THE WOUND IS DEEP...
THIS IS...!

KEEP THE AL-MIRAJ AT BAY, OUKA!
BA (WHIRL)
ON IT! I'M HEADING TO THE FRONT!
MIKOTO, WITH ME!
SIR!
GYO (SHUDDER)
!?

ZORO
ZORO (MASSING)
NOT GOOD...
A MON-STER PARTY!

ZA (RUSTLE)
HAA!
HAA!
HAA!
OUKA-DONO, WE MUST RETREAT!
BA (FWIP)
...ALL UNITS, WITHDRAW!

STEP 59 ▶▶ PASS PARADE

DA
DA
DA (DASH)
WHAT'S CHIGUSA-DONO'S CONDI-TION?
NOT GOOD.
THE POTIONS WE HAVE MAY SAVE HER.
HAA!
HAA!
BUT FIRST WE NEED TO PULL BACK TO FLOOR TWELVE WHERE WE CAN HEAL SAFE—
LOOK OUT!

OH NO!
MORE MONSTERS ON OUR TAIL!
DO (TMP)
DO
EVEN THE HELL-HOUNDS ARE CATCHING UP......!
DA

DA (DASH)
DA
DA
HURRY!
...!

ZA (WHOOSH)
!

DO (SLASH)
ZASHU (SLICE)
ARE THEY...A NEW FAMILIA IN THIS AREA?
...

...WE'RE CHARGING RIGHT THROUGH.
!?
OUKA-DONO, PLEASE WAIT!
IF WE DO, THOSE ADVENTURERS...!

I VALUE YOUR LIVES FAR MORE...
...THAN THOSE OF PEOPLE I DON'T KNOW.
...!

IF IT LEAVES A BAD TASTE IN YOUR MOUTH, YOU CAN SCOLD ME TO YOUR HEART'S CONTENT ONCE WE'RE OUT OF THIS.
HFF!
HAA!
HFF!
...!
GU (GRIMACE)
GI (CLENCH)
...I'M SO SORRY!
DADADA (RUSH)

...?
DO (TMP)
GRRRRRR!
GUO (HOWL)
GAHH!?
BA (FWIP)
ZUA (SHING)
DOO
GYARI (SLICE)
THAT WAS...
...TOO CLOSE...!

DO
DO
DO
DO
—!?
A HORDE OF MON-STERS ...!?
AH!

THIS IS BAD! IT'S A PASS PARADE!
THEY'VE USED US AS DECOYS!

DOOOOO

GA (CLANG)
GI (CLENCH)
BA (FWIP)
GACHIN (SNAP)

AGH!
DOO (SLAM)
ZUZAA (SLIDE)

LILLY!
DOO
ZAN (SLICE)
ZUA (FWISH)

ARE YOU OKAY!?
Y-YES...

SHOULD HAVE EXPECTED FASTER MONSTER SPAWN IN THE MIDDLE LEVELS.
ZAA (WHOOSH)
THERE ARE TOO MANY OF THEM...
HAA!
HAA!

BELL-SAMA, WELF-SAMA. LILLY HIGHLY RECOMMENDS A RETREAT.
IF WE DON'T FALL BACK AND REGROUP SOON...
I DON'T DIS-AGREE...
...PROBLEM IS WE'RE SUR-ROUNDED.
SO WE PICK A SIDE...
...AND FORCE OUR WAY THROUGH!
BA (THRUST)
BO (CRACKLE)
FIREBOLT!

GOO
GO
GOA (BOOM)

ALL RIGHT! LET'S GO!
DA
DA (TMP)
PLEASE MOVE QUICKLY! WE CAN'T AFFORD TO BE SUR-ROUNDED AGAIN!
EVEN IF WE CAN'T LOSE THEM, SOME DISTANCE WILL—
DA
DA
DA
BIGII (SPLIT)
BIKI
BIKI (CRACK)
BIKI

BAKIII
(CRUMBLE)

BIGI
(SPLIT)
BIGI
GII
WAAAAAHHHH!?
DOOOOOO
(BOOM)

OOOOO (RUMBLE)
HAA...
HAA...
GAH...
......
MISHI (GRIND)

GUGU (TENSE)
UGH...
ZULI (LOOM)

GOA
(BOOM)

IS it WRONG to TRY to PICK-UP GIRLS IN A DUNGEON?

GUILD

PETA (PRESS)
QUEST: "FIND BELL CRANELL AND HIS PARTY"
400000
8000

SOMETHING VERY BAD HAS HAP-PENED...
... HERMES-SAMA.

STEP 60 ▸▸ SUGGESTION AND DECISION

ONE HOUR EAR-LIER, GUILD
DADADA
DADA
DADA (ZOOM)
ADVISER-KUN!
BAN (POUND)
G-GOD-DESS HESTIA?
DID BELL-KUN COME THROUGH HERE YESTERDAY!?

J-JUST IN THE MORNING, BEFORE ENTERING THE DUN-GEON.
I HAVEN'T SEEN HIM SINCE THEN...
GU (SLUMP)
......
...HE DIDN'T COME HOME LAST NIGHT.
I HAVE NO IDEA WHERE BELL-KUN OR THE REST OF HIS PARTY IS.
NOT SINCE THEY WENT INTO THE DUNGEON...
BASASA (FLUTTER)
I...
...I SHALL ASK AROUND ......!
PLEASE WAIT HERE JUST A MOMENT!

TODAY'S THE DAY WE ENTER THE MIDDLE LEVELS!
YOU'LL BE CAREFUL, RIGHT? ALSO, LET ME KNOW IMMEDIATELY WHEN YOU GET BACK! GOT THAT?
OKAY!
BELL-KUN HASN'T BEEN BACK SINCE THEN.
I CAN'T JUST CASUALLY SIT BACK AND WAIT...!
MY HEAD, MY INTUITION—IT'S THROBBING.
WHEN BELL AND HIS PARTY TRIED TO LEAVE THE MIDDLE LEVELS...
...SOMETHING PROBABLY HAPPENED AND THEY FAILED.

SUU (SLIDE)
MY APOLOGIES FOR THE WAIT...
I CONTACTED THE DUNGEON'S EXCHANGE BUT...
...THEY HADN'T SEEN ANYONE WHO MATCHED BELL-KUN'S DESCRIPTION...
...!

...PLEASE, ADVISER-KUN...
...CAN YOU FIND OUT IF ANYONE HAS SEEN HIM?
AT ONCE!
YOU HAVE MY WORD THAT I WILL ASK AS MANY ADVENTURERS AS POSSIBLE.
ALSO—

I'D LIKE TO ISSUE A QUEST.
THE MISSION IS "FIND BELL AND HIS PARTY."
BAN (SMACK)

THERE'S NO TIME TO HOLD ANYTHING BACK.
I WANT ADVENTURERS ON THIS.
KA
KARI (SCRIBBLE)
KARI
WHAT DO YOU PROPOSE FOR THE *REWARD*?

FOUR HUNDRED THOUSAND VALIS.
MY FAMILIA'S ENTIRE SAVINGS.

UNDERSTOOD ...!

BA (STAND)
I WILL ASK FOR APPROVAL FROM UPSTAIRS IMMEDIATELY.
I WILL DO EVERYTHING IN MY POWER TO MAKE SURE IT'S ON THE BULLETIN BOARD AS FAST AS POSSIBLE...
PLEASE EXCUSE ME!

WHAT DID YOU FIND OUT ABOUT BELL AND HIS PARTY?
HESTIA!
NO LUCK. IT LOOKS LIKE THEY NEVER MADE IT OUT OF THE DUNGEON...
......

BUT, I KNOW BELL-KUN IS STILL ALIVE...!

THE FALNA I GAVE HIM...
MY BLESSING HASN'T DISAP-PEARED!
I KNOW, HESTIA.
PON (PAT)
THEY'RE ALL OKAY.
HESTIA-SAMA, HAVE YOU ALREADY APPLIED FOR A QUEST...?
YEAH. I MADE SURE TO FOLLOW EVERY PIECE OF ADVICE YOU GAVE ME, NAHZA-KUN.
THEN I SUGGEST WE PAY HEPHAISTOS AND TAKEMI-KAZUCHI A VISIT.

WE NEED AS MUCH HELP AS POSSIBLE.
OKAY!

TWENTY HOURS EARLIER —
GOOOO (HOOOOWL)
DUN-GEON

OOOO (FSSHHH)

HAA ...
ZA (TRAMP)
HAA ...
HAA ...
ZA
HAA ...
ZA
ZA

ZA
ZA
ZURI (DRAG)
ZURIRI
HAA...
HAA...
HAA...
ZA

BELL, LI'L E...
GIRI (GNASH)
FU (PANT)
FUU
IF WORSE COMES TO WORSE, DITCH ME...
WHY ARE YOU SAYING SOMETHING SO RIDICULOUS...?
HAA.
HAA.
HAA.
NO... ABSOLUTELY NOT...
HAA.
HAA.

... SORRY.

ZA (TRAMP)
ZA
ZA
ZA

WE WOULD HAVE BEEN WIPED OUT WITHOUT THE SAL-AMANDER WOOL...

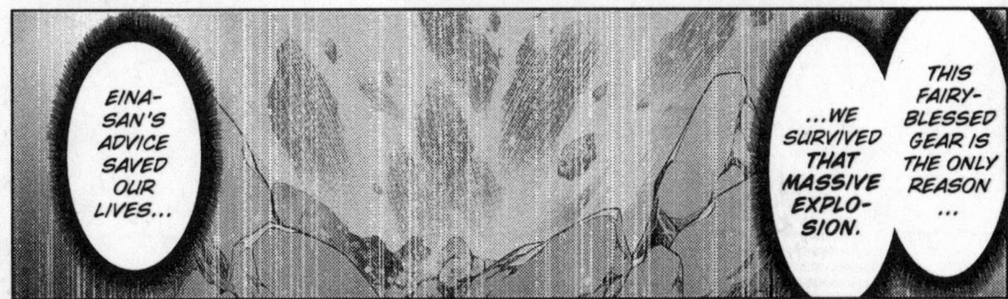
THIS FAIRY-BLESSED GEAR IS THE ONLY REASON ...
...WE SURVIVED THAT MASSIVE EXPLO-SION.
EINA-SAN'S ADVICE SAVED OUR LIVES...

THIS PLACE... I THINK IT'S THE FOUR-TEENTH FLOOR.
I RE-MEMBER BEING KNOCKED OFF MY FEET AFTER THE CEILING CAVED IN...
...AND ALL OF US FALLING DOWN A HOLE.
ZA
ZA
ZA
WE FELL FOR A DUNGEON GIMMICK.
IT'S WORSE THAN WE IMAGINED. THINGS LOOK BLEAK...
... ANOTHER ONE.

...!
ANOTHER DEAD END...

...
HAA.
TSK!
HAA.
HAA.
HAA.

FUU (EXHALE)
LET'S SETTLE DOWN FOR A MOMENT.
SU (TURN)

FIRST, WE SHOULD CHECK WHAT EQUIPMENT WE STILL HAVE.
LILLY HAS FOUR POTIONS AND TWO ANTI-DOTES.
BUT LOST THE BOW GUN DURING THE ROCK-SLIDE.

I GOT NOTHING BUT THAT GREAT-SWORD.
THOUGH, THE SAL-AMANDER WOOL STILL WORKS FINE.

I STILL HAVE A FEW POTIONS.
THE BROAD-SWORD, SHORT-SWORD, AND BUCKLER ARE GONE, BUT...
...I STILL HAVE THE HESTIA KNIFE AND USHI-WAKA-MARU.

UNDER-STOOD...
WITH SUCH MEAGER EQUIPMENT, FIGHTING MONSTERS WILL BE NEXT TO IMPOSSI-BLE.
AND UNDER THE CIRCUM-STANCES, WANDERING BLINDLY IS EXTREMELY DANGER-OUS...
WHICH BRINGS LILLY TO HER SUG-GESTION...
PLEASE LISTEN UNTIL THE END.

CONSIDERING HOW LONG WE WERE FALLING, WE LIKELY DROPPED TWO FLOORS.
THIS COULD VERY WELL BE FLOOR FIFTEEN.
GETTING TO THE SAFER UPPER LEVELS IS NEAR IMPOSSIBLE.
THEREFORE, LILLY SUGGESTS ...

...RATHER THAN TRYING TO GO UP...
ZA (SHF)
...!?
...GOING DOWN INSTEAD... AND TAKING SHELTER ON THE EIGHTEENTH FLOOR.

TAKE SHELTER ON THE EIGHTEENTH ...!?

FLOOR EIGHTEEN IS ONE OF THE FEW PLACES IN THE DUNGEON ***WHERE MONSTERS DON'T SPAWN***. IT IS A SAFE POINT.
ADVENTURERS PLANNING TO TRAVEL TO THE DEEP LEVELS ARE SAID TO USE IT AS A STAGING AREA. THEREFORE, LILLY BELIEVES WE'LL BE FREE FROM DANGER IF WE CAN MAKE IT THAT FAR.

STEP 61 ▶▶THE GOD'S DECISION

L-LILLY! WAIT A MINUTE! IF WE GO ANY LOWER THAN WE ARE NOW...!
WE'LL USE THE SHAFTS.

THERE ARE HUNDREDS OF THESE HOLES ALL AROUND THE MIDDLE LEVELS. WE CAN GO DOWN FLOORS BY JUMPING INTO ANY ONE OF THEM.
LILLY THINKS OUR CHANCE OF FINDING THEM IS MUCH BETTER THAN THE ONLY STAIRCASE GOING UP.

...WHAT ABOUT THE FLOOR BOSS?

IT'S THE SEVENTEENTH FLOOR, RIGHT? THAT'S WHERE THAT BIG GUY IS...
...MONSTER REX, GOLIATH.

THE DAY BELL-SAMA SLEW THAT MINOTAUR...
...WAS ABOUT TWO WEEKS AGO. LOKI FAMILIA'S EXPEDITION HAD JUST LEFT.

THE GOLIATH IS SAID TO RESIDE IN A LARGE CHAMBER JUST BEFORE THE ENTRANCE TO THE EIGHTEENTH FLOOR.
IT WOULD BE MORE EFFICIENT FOR A LARGE GROUP AS POWERFUL AS LOKI FAMILIA TO DEFEAT THE GOLIATH RATHER THAN AVOID IT.
LILLY IS CERTAIN THEY ELIMINATED IT.

THE GOLIATH HAS A TWO-WEEK RESPAWN INTERVAL ...
CONSIDERING THE TIME FRAME, THERE IS A POSSIBILITY THAT THE GOLIATH HAS YET TO BE REBORN.
YOU'RE SERIOUS ...?

...THIS IS ONLY AN OPTION.
THERE'S NO MISTAKE THAT RETURNING TO HIGHER FLOORS IS THE MORE CAREFUL ROUTE.
THERE'S ALSO A CHANCE TO ENCOUNTER ANOTHER PARTY ALONG THE WAY.
BUT THE MIDDLE LEVELS ARE QUITE LARGE, AND WE HAVEN'T SEEN OTHER ADVENTURERS SINCE WE FELL DOWN HERE...

JI (STARE)
BELL-SAMA, YOU ARE THE LEADER OF THIS BATTLE PARTY.
THE DECISION IS YOURS.
I AGREE.
IT'S YOUR CALL.
WHATEVER YOU CHOOSE, I WON'T HOLD IT AGAINST YOU.

...!!
DO (BADUM)

CHOOSE...
EVERYONE'S FATE IS IN MY HANDS...
WE'RE WORKING TOGETHER AS A PARTY, AND I'M THE LEADER.
LILLY AND WELF HAVE PUT THEIR TRUST IN ME...
I CAN'T RUN AWAY...
...FROM SOMETHING SO IMPORTANT...
(WOOSH)
LET'S KEEP GOING.

MIACH FAMILIA, "THE BLUE PHARMACY"
I MUST APOLOGIZE, HESTIA.
IT APPEARS THAT MY CHILDREN MAY BE THE REASON...
...YOURS HAVE NOT YET RETURNED.
THEY SAW SOMEONE FITTING HIS DESCRIPTION IN THE MIDDLE LEVELS...
...AND USED HIM AS A DECOY TO MAKE THEIR OWN ESCAPE...
...

IF BELL NEVER MAKES IT HOME...
...I'LL NEVER FORGIVE YOU.
SU (INHALE)
BUT I WILL NOT HATE YOU.
THAT I PROMISE.
FOR NOW, WOULD YOU BE WILLING TO LEND ME YOUR STRENGTH?
—AS YOU WISH.
ZAA (DROP)

HEPHAISTOS, CAN ANY OF YOUR CHILDREN JOIN THE SEARCH PARTY?
UNFORTUNATELY, MOST OF MINE ARE HELPING THE LOKI FAMILIA EXPEDITION...
ANY STRONG ENOUGH TO HELP ARE WITH THEM, I'M AFRAID.
THOSE AVAILABLE AT THE MOMENT WOULDN'T LAST LONG IN THE MIDDLE LEVELS.
SORRY.
NO... YOU DON'T HAVE TO APOLOGIZE.
THEN I SUGGEST WE PROCEED. TIME IS OF THE ESSENCE.
PAN (CLAP)
LOOKS LIKE WE'LL HAVE TO DEPEND ON YOURS, TAKÉ.
THAT'S FINE WITH ME...
OUKA AND MIKOTO WILL GO FOR SURE...
CHIGUSA, YOUR INJURIES HAVE HEALED, CORRECT?
CAN YOU ACCOMPANY THEM AS A SUPPORTER?
CHIRARI (GLANCE)
Y-YES!

THESE THREE ARE THE ONLY ONES OF MINE WHO CAN DEAL WITH MONSTERS IN THE MIDDLE LEVELS.
THE OTHERS WOULD JUST FALL BEHIND.
I THINK THE MOST IMPOR-TANT THING FOR A SEARCH PARTY IS SPEED...
NAHZA HAS A GOOD POINT.
IF WE SEND MORE PEOPLE FOR THE SAKE OF NUMBERS ONLY TO WEAKEN THE PARTY, WE'LL LOSE EVERYTHING AT STAKE.
HOWEVER, DEPENDING ON THESE THREE ALONE SEEMS...
WE DON'T HAVE ENOUGH PEOPLE.
DAMMIT... I'D GO MYSELF IF I COULD.

—I'LL JOIN YOU, HESTIA!
BIKU (FLINCH)

HEY THERE, HESTIA. LONG TIME.
NI (GRIN)
HERMES !?
WHY ARE YOU HERE...?
...!
BA (FWIP)
YOU'RE IN TROUBLE, AREN'T YOU?
YOU KNOW I'D PULL OUT ALL THE STOPS TO HELP A BUDDY IN NEED!

HERMES, HAVE YOU EVEN TALKED TO HESTIA SINCE SHE CAME DOWN FROM THE HEAVENS?
SOME FRIEND YOU ARE.
HA-HA! AREN'T WE BEING A LITTLE HARSH!?
BLANK STARE
SUU
BUT MY DESIRE TO HELP HER IS GENUINE.
—I, TOO, WANT TO SAVE BELL-KUN.
SO HOW ABOUT IT?
......

...FINE, THEN.
I'LL ACCEPT YOUR HELP, HERMES.
GREAT! YOU CAN COUNT ON ME!
GUKI (CRACK)
ARE YOU SURE ABOUT THIS, HESTIA?
RESCUING BELL AND HIS PARTY TAKES PRIORITY RIGHT NOW.
WE NEED PEOPLE.
BASHI (SLAP)
BASHI
INCLUDING HERMES'S FOLLOWERS IN THE SEARCH...
WILL THAT BE ENOUGH?
LAST I HEARD, MOST OF YOUR CHILDREN ARE LEVEL TWO, CORRECT?
I'M SORRY TO SAY MOST OF THEM ARE OUT ON BUSINESS, BUT I'M *TAKING ASFI WITH ME!*
SHE'S MY ACE, SO THERE'S NOTHING TO FEAR!
?

HERMES-SAMA...
JUST NOW, YOU SAID YOU ARE TAKING ME WITH YOU. DON'T TELL ME YOU'RE...
HISO HISO (WHISPER)
YUP.
I'M GOING TOO.
NIKOO (SMILE)
YOU WHAT!?
AREN'T DEITIES FOR-BIDDEN FROM ENTERING THE DUNGEON!?
THAT JUST MEANS I CAN'T BE CARE-LESS, RIGHT?
WHAT'S THE PROBLEM? I'LL BE BACK BEFORE THE GUILD EVEN NOTICES.

DON'T TELL ME THIS WAS YOUR PLAN ALL ALONG...!
HA-HA-HA! I'M COUNTING ON YOUR PROTEC-TION, ASFI!
HYU (WOOSH)
BAA (RISE)
GUGYUN (SNAG)
GHAH!?

A PIGTAIL!?
I CAN'T JUST SIT HERE AND WAIT ...
...WHILE OTHERS ARE OUT LOOKING FOR HIM.

—TAKE ME WITH YOU.

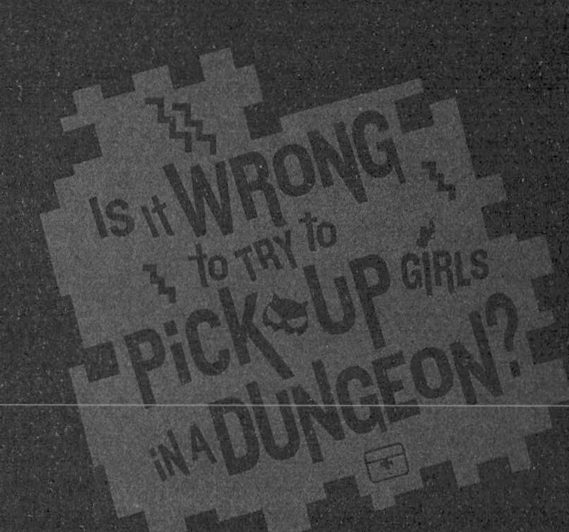
IS IT WRONG TO TRY TO PICK UP GIRLS IN A DUNGEON?

TAKE YOU WITH ME...!?
HAVE YOU LOST YOUR MIND!?
THE DUNGEON IS VERY DANGER-OUS.
WITHOUT ACCESS TO OUR DIVINE POWER, ONE HIT FROM A MONSTER AND WE'RE DONE.
BUT MOST OF ALL— IT'LL BE BAD IF WE'RE FOUND OUT.
I'M AWARE.
BUT IF YOU'RE STILL GOING, WHAT DIFFERENCE DOES AN EXTRA DEITY OR TWO MAKE?
WELL...
I'M COMING WITH YOU!
GOT IT?
STEP 62 ▸▸ GALE WIND RETURNS

SOMEHOW I'M NOT SUR-PRISED...
DON'T DO ANYTHING RECKLESS, OKAY?
I'LL BE FINE!
HMPH.
HESTIA-SAMA, HERE......
HEALING POTIONS. PLEASE TAKE THEM.
SORRY I CAN'T JOIN YOU...
THIS IS ALL I CAN DO TO HELP...
NO, THIS IS ENOUGH! THANKS, NAHZA-KUN!
I HAVE SOME-THING FOR YOU TOO.
SU (SLIDE)
OH?

WOAH!
ZUSHII (THUD)
SO HEAVY!!
H-HE-PHAIS-TOS, IS THIS ...?
BURU (SHAKE)
BURU
IT'S THAT CHILD, WELF'S CRE-ATION.
I'VE BEEN HOLDING ON TO IT FOR HIM.
YOU MAY USE IT IN A PINCH BUT...
...GIVE IT TO WELF IF YOU SEE HIM.
AND TELL HIM TO STOP WEIGHING HIS ALLIES' LIVES AGAINST HIS PRIDE.
SURE.
THIS COM-PLICATES THINGS...

MAYBE I SHOULD...
...CALL IN A LITTLE EXTRA HELP.

THE BENEVOLENT MISTRESS
SIGN: THE BENEVOLENT MISTRESS
...YOU WANT-ED TO SPEAK WITH ME?
YEP. I HAVE A FAVOR TO ASK...
...LYU-CHAN.
MORE SPECIFI-CALLY, A QUEST I'D LIKE YOU TO TAKE—
SU (STEP)

I NEED "LEON OF THE GALE WIND."
GISHI (SNAP)
ZO (SHUDDER)

ARE YOU IMPLYING THAT SHOULD I REFUSE YOUR REQUEST, YOU WILL GO PUBLIC WITH MY "TITLE"—
ARE YOU... THREATENING ME?
SU (RAISE)
THAT'S NOT MY INTEN-TION.
BELL-KUN...
THE QUEST IS TO ASSIST BELL CRANELL AND HIS PARTY MEMBERS.
...
WHAT DO YOU MEAN?

—SO THEN, CRANELL-SAN...
I DON'T KNOW ENOUGH TO SAY FOR SURE AT THIS POINT.
BUT I'D LIKE YOU TO JOIN THE SEARCH PARTY, LYU-CHAN.
WHY DID YOU COME TO ME?
THERE'S SOME "BAGGAGE" THAT NEEDS PROTEC-TION.
AND I NEED A STRONG ADVENTURER NOT BOUND BY THE RULES OF A FAMILIA. YOU'RE THE ONLY ONE I COULD THINK OF...
AND...
...BECAUSE YOU'RE SYR-CHAN'S FRIEND, MAYBE?

...!
NI (GRIN)
WE SET OUT AT EIGHT O'CLOCK TONIGHT.
JOIN US. WE'LL BE WAITING FOR YOU.

TA (RUN) TA

LYU.
SYR...

...!
...
SORRY.
LYU...
...PLEASE SAVE BELL-SAN.
...
I AM IN YOUR DEBT, SYR.
I CANNOT REFUSE YOUR RE-QUEST.
MORE-OVER ...
...I DO NOT WANT CRANELL-SAN TO DIE EITHER.

SORRY. I'M SO SORRY...
THANK YOU.
LEAVE THE BAR TO US, MEOW.
DON'T WORRY ABOUT MAMA MIA EITHER. WE'LL TRICK HER SOME-MEOW!
IRRITATING AS IT IS TO DO AS HERMES-SAMA SAYS, IT CAN'T BE HELPED, MEOW...
SAVE THE BOY AND HE'LL OWE YOU, MEOW!
BISHI (SNAP)
...MY APOLOGIES.

PLEASE COVER FOR ME.
SHURU (WHOOSH)
BA (TURN)

EIGHT HOURS HAVE PASSED SINCE THEIR FATEFUL DECISION...
ZARI
ZA (STEP)
ZARI (STAGGER)

ZA
ZA
BELL'S CURRENT LOCATION: FLOOR FIFTEEN—

IS it WRONG
to TRY to
PICK-UP GIRLS
IN A DUNGEON?

DUNGEON FLOOR FIFTEEN
HAA... HAA...

ZA (SLOG)
HAA... HAA...
ZARI (STUMBLE)
ZA
STEP 63 ▸▸ DEPARTURE
...! LI'L E...

THIS SMELL!
CAN'T YOU DO SOMETHING ABOUT IT!?
BA (GASP)
PLEASE TOLERATE IT.
MUWAA (WAFT)
LILLY WOULD LIKE TO MENTION THE *STENCH* IS MUCH WORSE BACK HERE.

THIS MALBORO STINK BOMB MAY BOTHER US...
...BUT IT'S LIKE BREATHING POISON FOR MON-STERS.
FUUUUN (FWSHHH)
THEREFORE, NONE WILL COME NEAR US AS LONG AS NOTHING HAPPENS...
THE EFFECT IS STRONGER THAN I THOUGHT.
UGH ...
IT MAY SMELL HOR-RIBLE BUT...
...I'M GLAD WE HAVE IT.

THERE'S NO ROOM FOR ANY ERROR RIGHT NOW.
GETTING ATTACKED WOULD BE DISAS-TROUS...

...!
HELL-HOUNDS!
ZA (JUMP)

BOU (FWOOSH)

THEIR FIRE BREATH!
THEY CAN ATTACK WITHOUT GETTING CLOSE TO THE MALBORO SMELL...!

GOAAA (RUMBLE)
FIRE-BOLT'S THE ONLY—
NO, HELL-HOUNDS RESIST FIRE...!

LOOKS LIKE I'M UP...
HUH?
I GOT THIS.

BLAS-
PHEMOUS
BURN.
ZUA
(FWISH)
BUOO
(WHOOSH)

GOGOA
(BA-BOOM)
WILL-O'-THE-WISP.
IGNIS FATUUS!?

GOOOOO (WOOSH)
HOW ABOUT THAT? IT WORKED...
W-WELF? WHAT WAS THAT JUST NOW?

WILL-O'-THE-WISP. ...MY MAGIC.
IT'S A BIT OF A SPECIAL-TY.
IT'S LIKE A SPARK THAT CAUSES A MAGICAL REACTION, MAKING MAGIC ENERGY EXPLODE.
HAA...
HAA...
HA...

ANTI-MAGIC FIRE.
IT MAKES TARGETS DETONATE BY TRIGGERING IGNIS FATUUS—EFFECTIVELY SEALING MAGIC ENERGY...
THAT'S AMAZING.
I TRIED USING IT IN THAT BATTLE EARLIER BUT...
...THE ROCK-SLIDE THREW OFF MY TIMING.

ほわあ
WHOA!

...ANY-WAY...
...I ONLY MANAGED IT BY THE SKIN OF MY TEETH.
HAA!
HAA!

ガくん
GAKUN (WOBBLE)
!?
WELF, YOU OKAY!?
...FINE.
BEEN SO LONG SINCE I USED MAGIC, TOOK A LOT OUT OF ME...

HA...
HAAA...

WELF, HERE...
SU (PULL)
MAGIC POTION? SORRY TO TROUBLE YOU...
GUI (GLUG)
APPRECI-ATE IT...
!

A DUAL POTION!?
SU (PASS)
IT'S NAHZA'S LATEST CONCOCTION...
THIS IS GOOD STUFF.
GUI
I FEEL LIGHTER!
...B-BELL-SAMA, SHARE A POTION WITH LILLY TOO.
DOKI
DOKI (BADUM)
I JUST DRANK SOME SO I'M OKAY.
WE DON'T WANT TO WASTE IT.
NO FAIR! IT'S NO FAIR THAT ONLY WELF-SAMA GETS TO!
KUWAA (YELL)
?
?

MAKING GOOD MEMORIES WITHOUT LILY...!
SERIOUSLY, WHAT ARE YOU TALKING ABOUT?
!

DUNGEON GIMMICK— SHAFTS LEADING DEEPER UNDER-GROUND
OOOO (SHHHHH)
FOUND ONE...

THIS PIT...
...WITHOUT A DOUBT CONNECTS TO A LOWER FLOOR.
JUDGING BY ITS DEPTH... PROBABLY GOES TO THE SIXTEENTH.

GUI (CLENCH)
GASSHI (GRAB)
KOKU (NOD)
BA (LEAP)

EIGHT O'CLOCK, BABEL TOWER, WESTGATE, CENTRAL PARK
TA (TMP)
TA
TA
SORRY TO KEEP YOU WAIT-ING.
YOU BETTER BE, HERMES!
KA (RAGE)

HAD MINOR BUSINESS TO TAKE CARE OF, OR MAYBE CALL IT A FORMALI-TY...
...THIS AND THAT, YOU KNOW.

?
WHAT-EVER! NOW WE'RE ALL HERE, YES?
IT'S ABOUT TIME WE GOT—

HESTIA-SAMA...!

!
SU (SHF)

...!
BA
(GRAB)

—GLAD YOU'LL BE JOINING US!
HM?

... HERMES?

I ASKED HER TO COME ALONG.
FAILED TO MENTION THAT.
NO NEED TO WORRY.

LYU-CHAN'S HERE TO HELP...
...AND IS VERY STRONG.
WOW...
ZA (STEP)

...ALL RIGHT.
LET'S BE ON OUR WAY.
SEARCH PARTY, MOVING IN!

STEP 64 ▸▸ ANOTHER CONFRONTATION

DUNGEON "MIDDLE LEVELS" FLOOR THIRTEEN
GWAH!
KYUI!
BUN (THROW)
GYARU (SPIN)
RURU (WHIRL)
PASHI (SNATCH)
GYUN (FLING)
ZUGAA (CRASH)
GAKUN (SPLAT)

I SHALL REMAIN HERE TO PROTECT HERMES-SAMA.
THEY'RE ALL YOURS.
ZA (AWE)
UNDER-STOOD.
DA (DASH)
GU (SET)

GOGOO (KABOOM)
GUN (STRETCH)
ZAN (SHING)
GOHHYA (KA-THUNK)
ZUGAA (CRASH)

DO (BURST)
SHE SHOULD BE FINE ON HER OWN AS THE POINT PERSON.
WELL, LESS WORK FOR ME.
BIKIKI (CRACK)
BIKI
BOGOO (CRASH)

BA (PULL)
PAAN (SHATTER)
PASHAN (PLINK)
BASHA (SPLASH)
MIRII (TWIST)
GI (CREAK)
MISHII (WARP)
!
...!!
GISHI (GROAN)
DA (FWIP)

ZOBUU (CARVE)
BUSHAA (SLIDE)
I SHOULD BE MORE THAN ENOUGH TO COVER OUR BACK.
ZUSHAA (SPURT)
TH-THEY'RE BOTH... SO STRONG...!
... HER-MES.
AREN'T YOUR FOLLOWERS LEVEL TWO ON AVER-AGE?
JITO (STARE)
HA-HA-HA! NOW THAT YOU MENTION IT, I FORGOT TO REPORT HER LEVEL-UP!

AT LEAST WE DON'T HAVE TO WORRY ABOUT ANYTHING ALONG THE WAY.
THERE'D BE NO POINT IF WE GET ALL FLUSTERED.
KACHAN (CLACK)
HUH?
DID I STEP ON SOME-THING —?

EEEEK!?
M-M-MON-STERS HERE TOO!?

EASY NOW, HESTIA.
THIS ONE'S ALREADY DEAD.
CALM DOWN.
I-IT IS...?

JUDGING BY ITS CONDI-TION, I'D SAY IT'S BEEN DEAD A WHILE.
THE ADVENTUR-ER WHO SLEW IT MUST NOT HAVE HAD ENOUGH TIME TO COLLECT ITS MAGIC STONE...
I SEE... THE MIDDLE LEVELS REALLY ARE DIF-FERENT.
...ASFI, WHERE SHOULD WE START LOOKING?
SEARCHING HAPHAZ-ARDLY WON'T GET US ANY-WHERE.
...!
STAY SAFE, BELL-KUN...!
TRUE ...

THEY ENTERED THE DUNGEON LIGHTLY EQUIPPED BUT HAVE SPENT OVER A DAY IN THE MIDDLE LEVELS...
BUT THAT NORMALLY WOULDN'T MAKE ANY SENSE.
SOME-THING MUST'VE FORCED THEIR HAND... PERHAPS THEY FELL INTO ONE OF THE SHAFTS?
OPTIONS FOR PARTIES IN SUCH A SITUATION ARE LIMITED...
ABANDONING THOUGHTS OF RETURNING TO THE SURFACE AND TRYING TO REACH THE SAFETY OF FLOOR EIGHTEEN...
...I BELIEVE THAT THOUGHT PROCESS HAS MERIT.
...WOULD THEY REALLY DO THAT?
A DECISION LIKE THAT TAKES SERIOUS GUTS.
I WOULD.
バッ
BA (GASP)
HE HAS ALREADY OVERCOME ONE "AD-VENTURE"—
I BELIEVE HE WOULD PRESS FORWARD WITHOUT LOOKING BACK.

DUNGEON "MIDDLE LEVELS" FLOOR SIXTEEN
PLEASE WAIT!

HUH ...?
LILLY, WHAT'S WRONG?

...!
THE MALBORO RAN OUT...

...!
ZUN (DUN)
ZOA (SHUDDER)

EH...
TH...?
TH-THIS FEELING... SOMETHING MURDEROUS ...!?
PORO (DROP)
ポロッ

BA (WHOOSH)

ZUDOO (BAM)
GO (STOMP)

MINOTAUR!!
ブフォッ
BUFUO (SNORT)

UUWWOOOOOHHH!

BIRI
BIRI
BIRI
BIRI
BIRI (TREMBLE)
ZUA (FLASH)
—DEATH!
—!

BUO (ROAR)
!?
DAN (BAM)
DAN
BUA (WHOOSH)
STEP 65 ▸▸ HERO'S WILD DANCE

DOO
(ZOOM)
VAA
(WHOOSH)
HAAA!!

ZUZAA (SCREECH)
BUSYU (GUSH)
GUH
BA (SHING)

GYARU (SPIN)
BUO (WHOOSH)
ZUA (SHING)
DO (THUD)
ZAN (SLASH)
GOA (WHAM)
DO

GYLN
(SWING)

ZUA
(SLASH)

UGH...
KH...
GUAH...
DO (THUD)
DOO
DOO
FUU (PANT)
FUU
FUU
BOTA
BOTA (DRIP)
BA (WHIP)
GURA (STAGGER)

ZUZUN
(COLLAPSE)
...!

GU
(GRAB)

ZUSHI
(THUMP)

UHAA!
UGHA, HA, A-
DODOO (THUD)
DO
DO
DO
DO
DODOO

RIN (RING)
RIN
OOOOO (ROOOAR)
GU (LIFT)

RIN
VUVO (GROWL)
RIN
RIN
BUA (CHARGE)

GOGOO (KABOOM)

PARA
パ
PARA
パ
PARA (FLUTTER)
パ
...!
O—
—OX SLAYER.

Is it WRONG to TRY to PiCK UP GIRLS iN A DUNGEON?

DUN-GEON FLOOR THIR-TEEN
I THINK IT'S ABOUT TIME YOU CAME CLEAN, HERMES.
WHAT'S THE REAL REASON YOU WANT TO HELP BELL-KUN?
HEY, HEY. I AL-READY TOLD YOU!
WHEN A BUDDY OF MINE NEEDS HELP—
THAT LINE'S NOT GOING TO WORK ANY-MORE!
WE'VE ALREADY COME THIS FAR, SO DROP THE ACT!!
I WANT A STRAIGHT ANSWER, HERMES!
ZA (STEP)
...
I HEAR YOU, HESTIA.
STEP 66 ▸▸ A NEW CONQUEST

I CAME BACK FROM MY TRIP EARLY...
...BECAUSE A CERTAIN SOMEONE ASKED ME TO CHECK UP ON BELL-KUN.
A CERTAIN SOME-ONE?
THE ONE WHO RAISED HIM.
OR SO HE CLAIMS.
...BELL-KUN'S GRAND-FATHER IS DEAD, ISN'T HE?
SOME-THING UNAVOID-ABLE CAME UP.
HE'S BEEN HEARING A LOT ABOUT THE BOY BUT CAN'T GO INVES-TIGATE FOR HIMSELF.
MEAN-WHILE, SEEING HOW I GO IN AND OUT OF ORARIO ALL THE TIME, I OFFERED MY SER-VICES.
...SO, WHICH GOD IS USING YOU AS AN ERRAND BOY? DON'T TELL ME IT'S—
I NEVER SAID MY CLIENT WAS A GOD, NOW, DID I?
......
NI (GRIN)
BEFORE HE COULD EXPLAIN ANYTHING TO HIS PRECIOUS GRAND-SON...
...HE HAD TO FAKE HIS OWN DEATH AND HAS BEEN IN HIDING EVER SINCE.
...I UNDER-STAND YOUR SITUA-TION.
BUT THERE'S NO NEED FOR YOU TO COME INTO THE DUN-GEON...
THERE WERE PLENTY OF OTHER WAYS TO HELP, RIGHT?

I MAY BE DOING SOME-ONE A FAVOR...
...BUT I AM INTER-ESTED IN BELL-KUN TOO.
ZUI (SHUDDER)
I WANT TO SEE WHAT HE'S CAPABLE OF WITH MY OWN EYES, HESTIA.
KNOW IF HE HAS WHAT IT TAKES—
...TO BE A HERO WHO CAN SHOULDER THIS ERA.

DUNGEON FLOOR SIXTEEN
DOOAAA (WHOOSH)
GOO (BOOM)
!?
GAKU (SLUMP)
WELF!
KUH...
MIND DOWN!
WE'VE BEEN RELYING ON HIS MAGIC TOO MUCH...
...AH.
LILLY!
ZUSHA (SLIDE)

I'M SURE SHE'S BEEN RUNNING ON FUMES FOR A WHILE NOW.
EVEN THOUGH SHE HAS THE LOWEST STATUS OF ALL OF US...
...SHE PRIOR-ITIZED GIVING US HEALING ITEMS WITHOUT TAKING ANY HER-SELF...
I WON'T LET THEM DIE...
GU (GRAB)
I WON'T...!
GUN (LIFT)
ALL OF US ARE MAKING IT OUT OF HERE ALIVE...!
ZA (MARCH)
BEFORE MON-STERS FIND US...
...I GOTTA FIND ANOTHER SHAFT...
ZA
ZA

—GH!
EVERYTHING FEELS SO HEAVY...
WIELDING THAT MUCH POWER WITHOUT A PRICE...
HA...
HA...
HA...
ARGONAUT... I USED A TON OF PHYSICAL AND MENTAL ENERGY WITH THAT SKILL DURING THE LAST BATTLE...
...THERE'S NO WAY SOMETHING LIKE THAT'S POSSIBLE!
OOOOOO (FSSSHHH)
—I DON'T EVEN KNOW HOW LONG WE'VE BEEN WANDERING AROUND THE DUNGEON.

MY FRIEND CAN'T HE ME RIG NOW.
WE DON'T HAVE ANY MAGIC POTIONS OR DUAL POTIONS LEFT.
I HAVE TO DO IT ALONE.
DID IT GET DARKER?
...NO. THE DUNGEON'S THE SAME AS ALWAYS.
THIS IS MY MIND PLAYING TRICKS ON ME.
FEAR.
WORRY.
DESPAIR.
MY HEART FEELS HEAVY... MY LEGS REFUSE TO MOVE...
...AND—

DON'T...
...MESS WITH ME ...!!
GI (GRIT)
GU (CLENCH)
HA.

...I FOUND ONE.
OOOOO (SHHHHH)
A SHAFT...

DAN (JUMP)

HYUOOOOO (WHOOSH)

—OOF!?
ZUDAN (SLAM)
ZAZA
ZAZAZAA (TUMBLE)

UGH ... GAH ...
GUGU (GROAN)

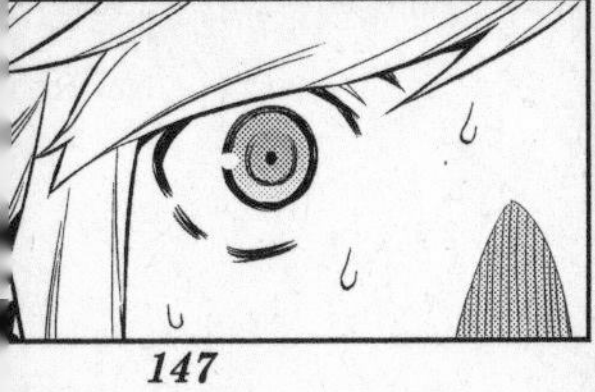

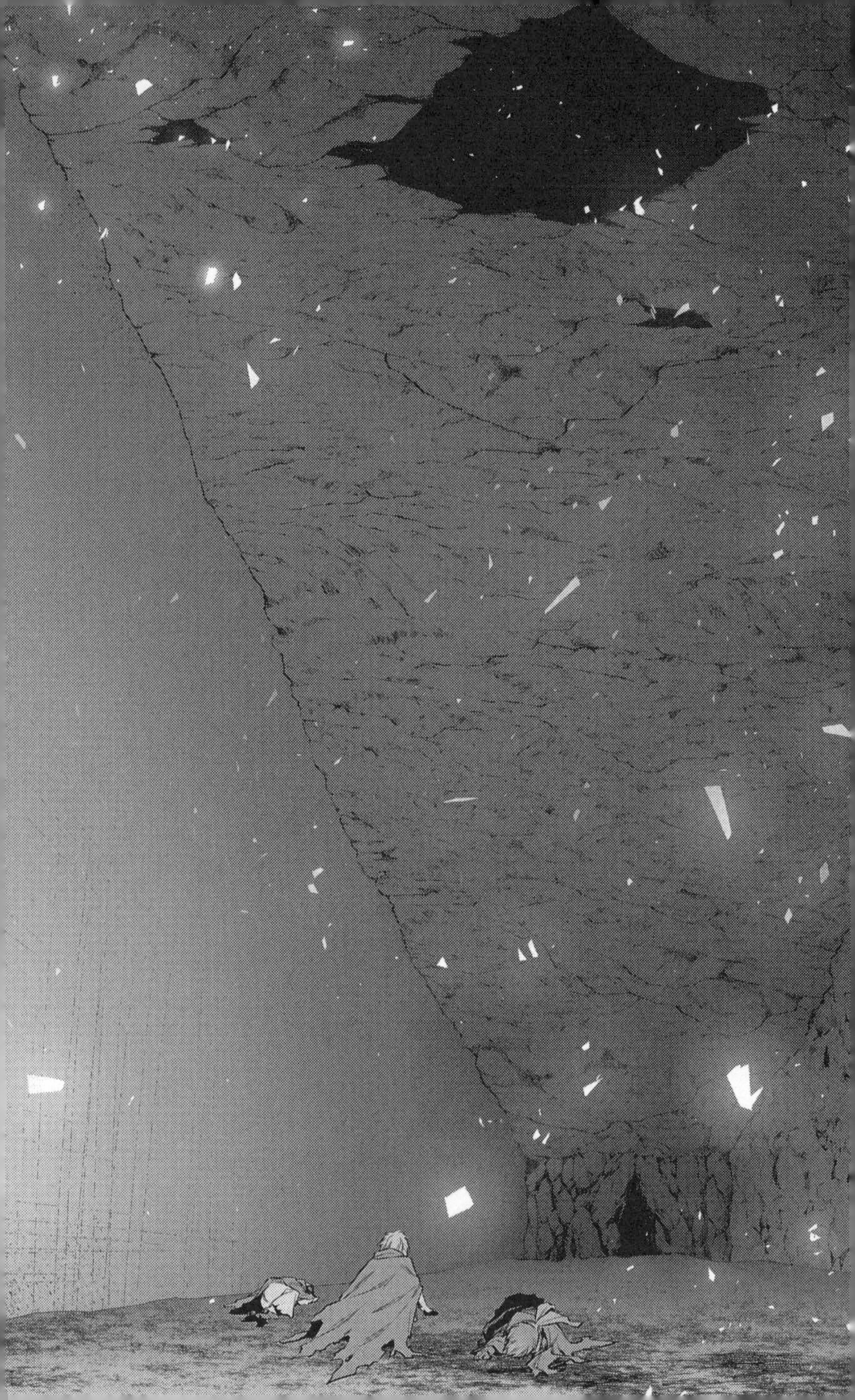

THAT'S—
...THE GREAT WALL OF SORROWS.

MONSTER REX... THIS IS THE LAST PART OF FLOOR SEVENTEEN, WHERE THE FLOOR BOSS IS BORN...!
ZOKU (SHUDDER)
BUT THE FLOOR BOSS...
...ISN'T HERE?
LILLY WAS RIGHT. LOKI FAMILIA MUST'VE TAKEN CARE OF IT...!

THAT MEANS... THAT'S THE ENTRANCE TO THE EIGHTEENTH FLOOR...!?

BIKI (CRACK)
BIKUN (JOLT)

GUGU (LIFT)
HAVE TO HURRY...
THIS IS THE FINAL STRETCH ...!

ZA (STAND)
HAA!
HAA!

BUKI (CRICK)
MEKIKI (SPLIT)
BIKI
BIKI
BIKIKI
BIGI! (SHATTER)

GOA
(ROAR)

GOGO (CRUMBLE)
ZUKI (CRUMBLE)

A MONSTER REX—
GOLIATH.

DA (DASH)
R-RUN...
GOTTA RUN!
RUN!!

PLEASE!
SAVE MY FRIENDS ...!

STEP 67 ▶▶ ARRIVAL

......
...NH?
ボー...
BOO (GROGGY)

AH!

LILLY!
GABA (BOLT)
WELF!?
ZUKIN (ZING)
~~~!?
GURA (LIMP)
MUNYU (POMF)
HUH?
ARE YOU OKAY?
~~~

EH!?
HUH!
A-
AIZ-
SAN!?
E-
EHH!?
ぱっ
BA
(JOLT)
SORRY!?
WH-
WHY
ARE
YOU
HERE
...!?
WE'RE RETURNING HOME FROM OUR EXPEDITION... AND STOPPED ON THIS FLOOR...
...USING THE SAFE POINT TO REST AND RECOVER.
THE THREE OF YOU FELL OUT OF THE FLOOR ENTRANCE...
YOUR INJURIES WERE TERRIBLE, SO...
!
AH!
WHERE ARE THEY—!?

THEY'RE BOTH FINE...
RIVERIA AND THE OTHERS HEALED THEM.
SUU (ZZZ)
SUU
SUKA (SNORE)

LILLY...
WELF...
THANK GOOD-NESS...

YOU WERE IN VERY BAD SHAPE TOO...
FEELING FINE?
OH!
UH, I-I...!
THANK YOU SO MUCH... FOR RESCU-ING US...
...I'M GLAD.
YOU LOOK OKAY.

SUKA (STAND)
KAAAA (BLUSH)
FINN ...
...OUR CAPTAIN ASKED ME TO REPORT TO HIM.
ZAA (SHF)
COULD YOU COME WITH ME?

SO THIS IS THE PARTY OF LOKI FAMILIA ADVENTURERS...
...SAID TO BE THE BEST IN ALL ORARIO...

GOGO (RUMBLE)
GO
GO
GO
AH HA.

WHAT'S WITH ALL OF THESE DEATH STARES...?
COULDN'T BE BECAUSE AIZ HAS BEEN TAKING CARE OF ME, COULD IT!?
BURURI (SHIVER)
?

!
SAAA (SHINE)

WHAT'S WRONG?

OH, NO, UM...
THIS IS THE EIGH-TEENTH FLOOR... WE'RE IN THE DUNGEON, RIGHT?
WHY IS IT SO BRIGHT ...?
...

...SHALL WE TAKE A DETOUR?

WOW ...
ZA (STEP)

...AMAZING.

—TH-THIS
IS...!?

YES...
...ALL CRYSTAL.

THE LIGHT FROM THE CRYSTALS FADES AS TIME PASSES ...
...AND "NIGHT" COMES.
THE EIGHTEENTH FLOOR IS A WORLD OF ITS OWN, FILLED WITH CRYSTALS AND NATURE.
......
WE'RE SAVED...

IS IT WRONG TO TRY TO PICK UP GIRLS IN A DUNGEON? 8 END

THANK YOU FOR PURCHASING VOLUME 8 OF THE MANGA SERIES!

THE *SWORD ORATORIA* ANIME IS ABOUT TO BEGIN! AIZ DIDN'T HAVE MUCH PRESENCE IN THIS VOLUME, BUT SHE SHOWS WHY SHE'S BELL'S IDOL IN *SWORD ORATORIA*!

ADDITIONALLY, LYU'S SIDE STORY HAS BEEN PUBLISHED AS BOTH A LIGHT NOVEL AND AS A COMIC. I SUPPOSE IT COULDN'T BE HELPED—LYU IS JUST THAT AWESOME.

THE WORLD OF DUNGEON KEEPS GETTING LARGER. KEEP GOING STRONG, DUNGEON!

I MUST KEEP GROWING RIGHT ALONG WITH IT.

JOIN ME IN THE NEXT VOLUME!

IS IT WRONG TO TRY TO PICK UP GIRLS IN A DUNGEON? ⑧

Fujino Omori
Kunieda
Suzuhito Yasuda

Translation: Andrew Gaippe • Lettering: Brndn Blakeslee

Yen Press
1290 Avenue of the Americas
New York, NY 10104

Visit us at yenpress.com
facebook.com/yenpress
twitter.com/yenpress
yenpress.tumblr.com
instagram.com/yenpress

First Yen Press Edition: November 2017

Yen Press is an imprint of Yen Press, LLC.
The Yen Press name and logo are trademarks of Yen Press, LLC.

The publisher is not responsible for websites (or their content) that are not owned by the publisher.

Library of Congress Control Number: 2015288171

ISBNs: 978-0-316-41190-5 (paperback)
978-0-316-41191-2 (ebook)

10 9 8 7 6 5 4 3 2 1

BVG

Printed in the United States of America